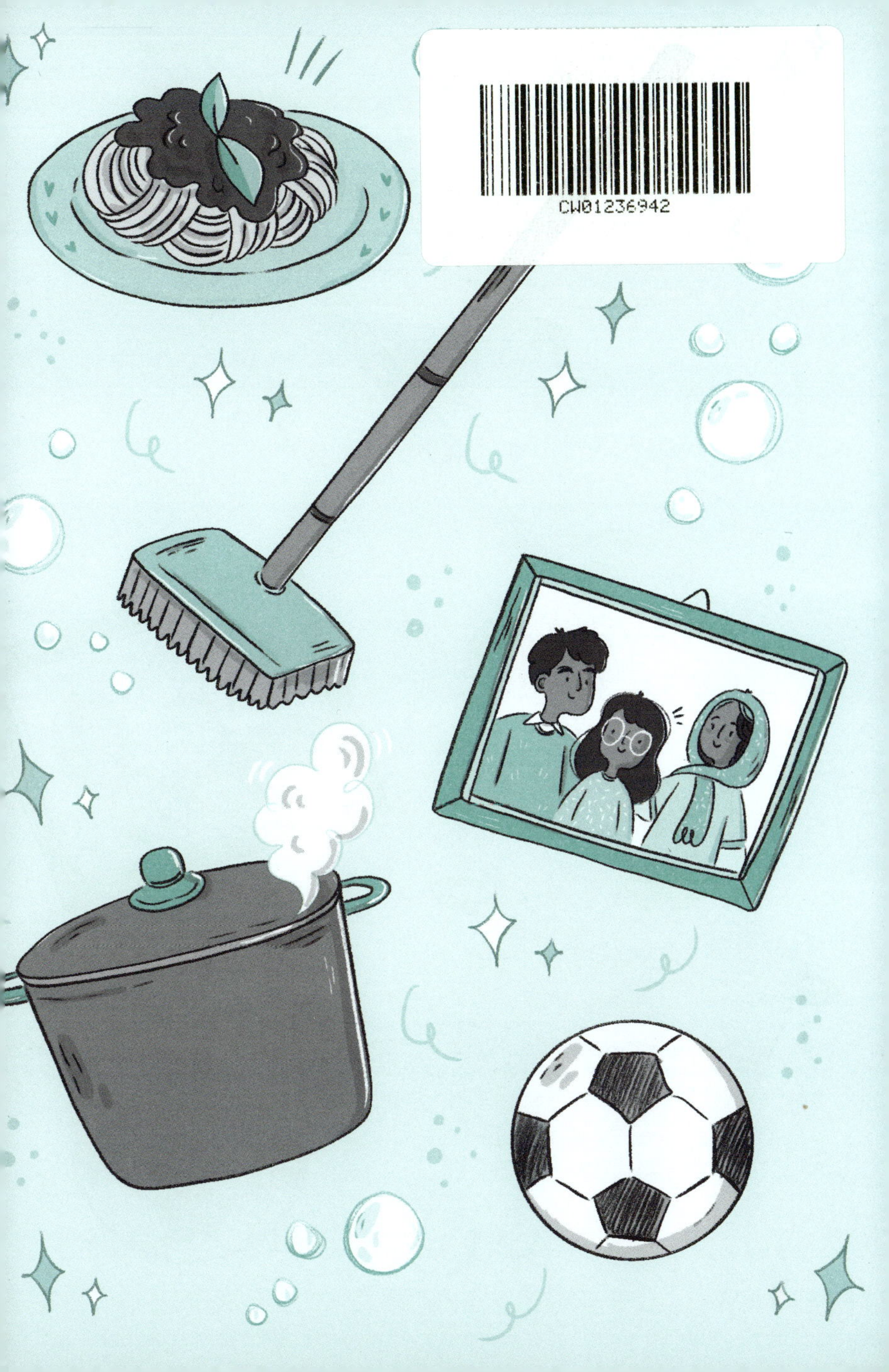

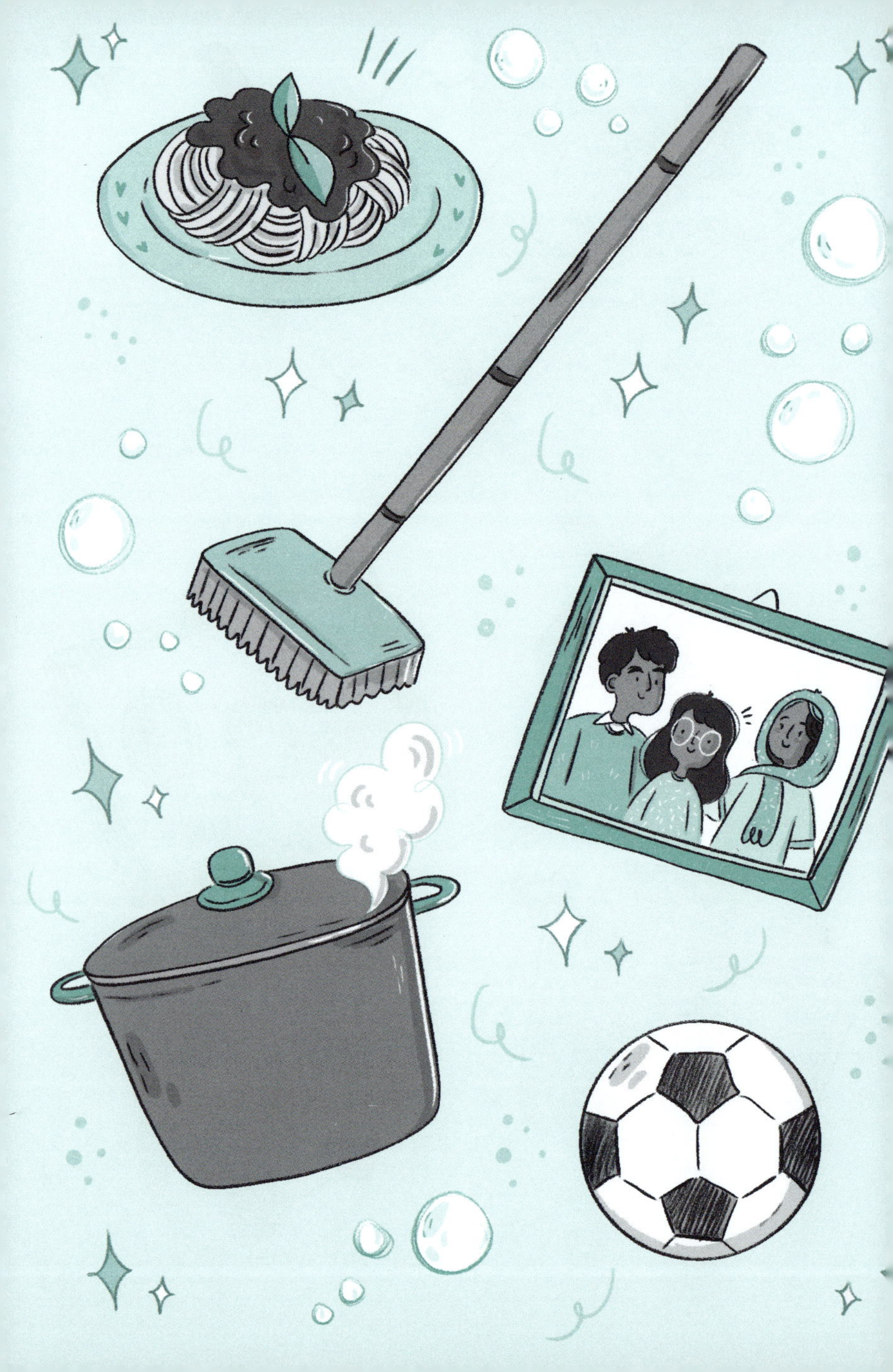

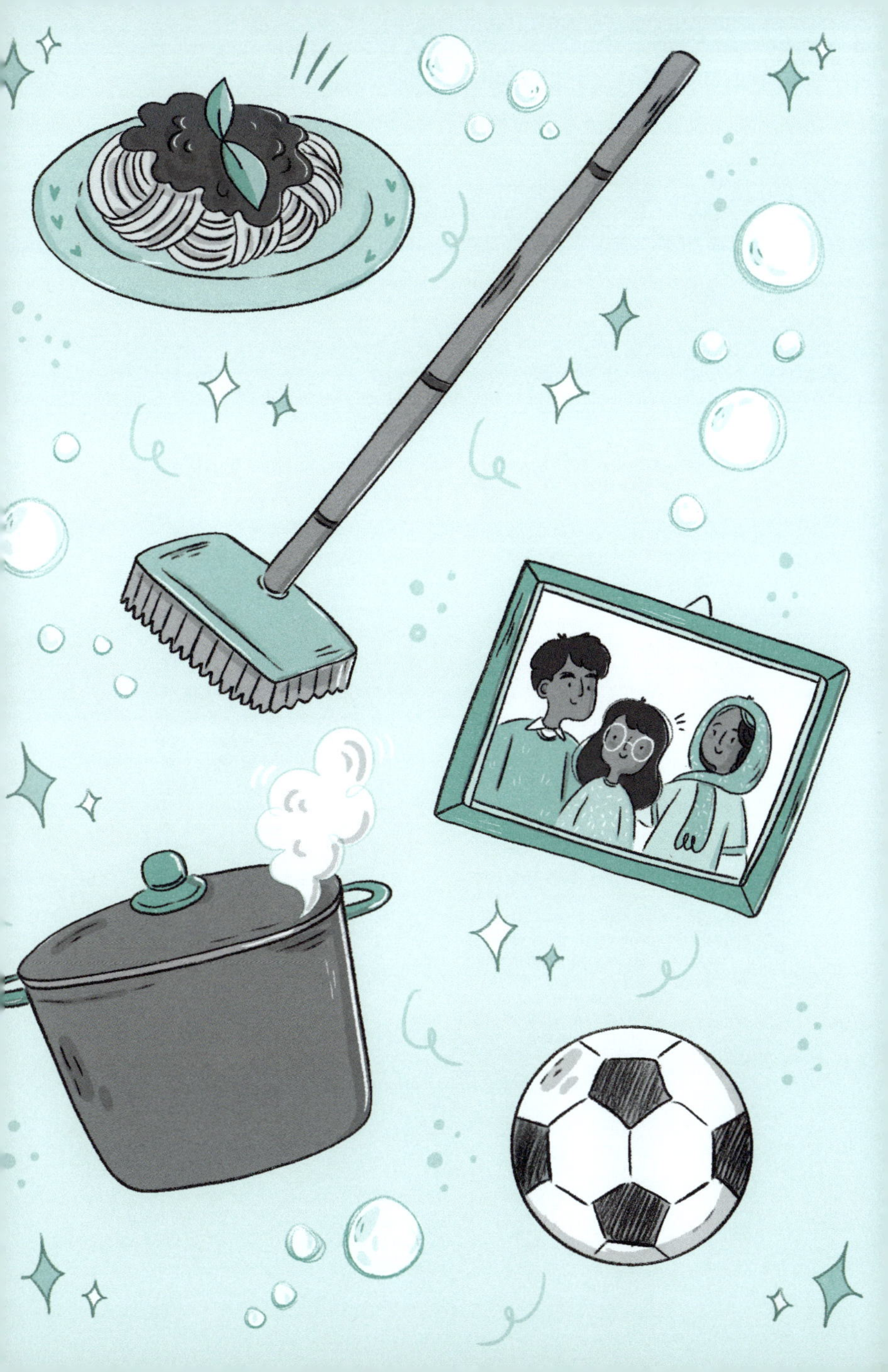

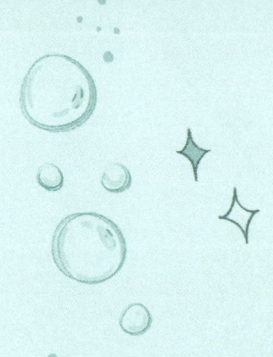

OXFORD
UNIVERSITY PRESS

Great Clarendon Street, Oxford, OX2 6DP,
United Kingdom

Oxford University Press is a department of the University of Oxford. It furthers the University's objective of excellence in research, scholarship, and education by publishing worldwide. Oxford is a registered trade mark of Oxford University Press in the UK and in certain other countries

Text © Oxford University Press 2024

Illustrations © Irma Ruggiero 2024

The moral rights of the author have been asserted

First Edition published in 2024

All rights reserved. No part of this publication may be reproduced, stored in a retrieval system, or transmitted, in any form or by any means, without the prior permission in writing of Oxford University Press, or as expressly permitted by law, by licence or under terms agreed with the appropriate reprographics rights organization. Enquiries concerning reproduction outside the scope of the above should be sent to the Rights Department, Oxford University Press, at the address above.

You must not circulate this work in any other form and you must impose this same condition on any acquirer

British Library Cataloguing in Publication Data

Data available

ISBN: 978-1-382-04371-7

10 9 8 7 6 5 4 3 2 1

The manufacturing process conforms to the environmental regulations of the country of origin.

Printed in China by Golden Cup

Acknowledgements

The Pasta Prank and Talking to a Friend written by Sufiya Ahmed

Content on pages 9, 23, 37, 50, 63, 86, 88 and 92 written by Suzy Ditchburn

Illustrated by Irma Ruggiero

Author photo courtesy of Sufiya Ahmed

Every effort has been made to contact copyright holders of material reproduced in this book. Any omissions will be rectified in subsequent printings if notice is given to the publisher.

MIX
Paper | Supporting responsible forestry
FSC www.fsc.org FSC™ C110497

The Pasta Disaster

Written by Sufiya Ahmed
Illustrated by Irma Ruggiero

OXFORD
UNIVERSITY PRESS

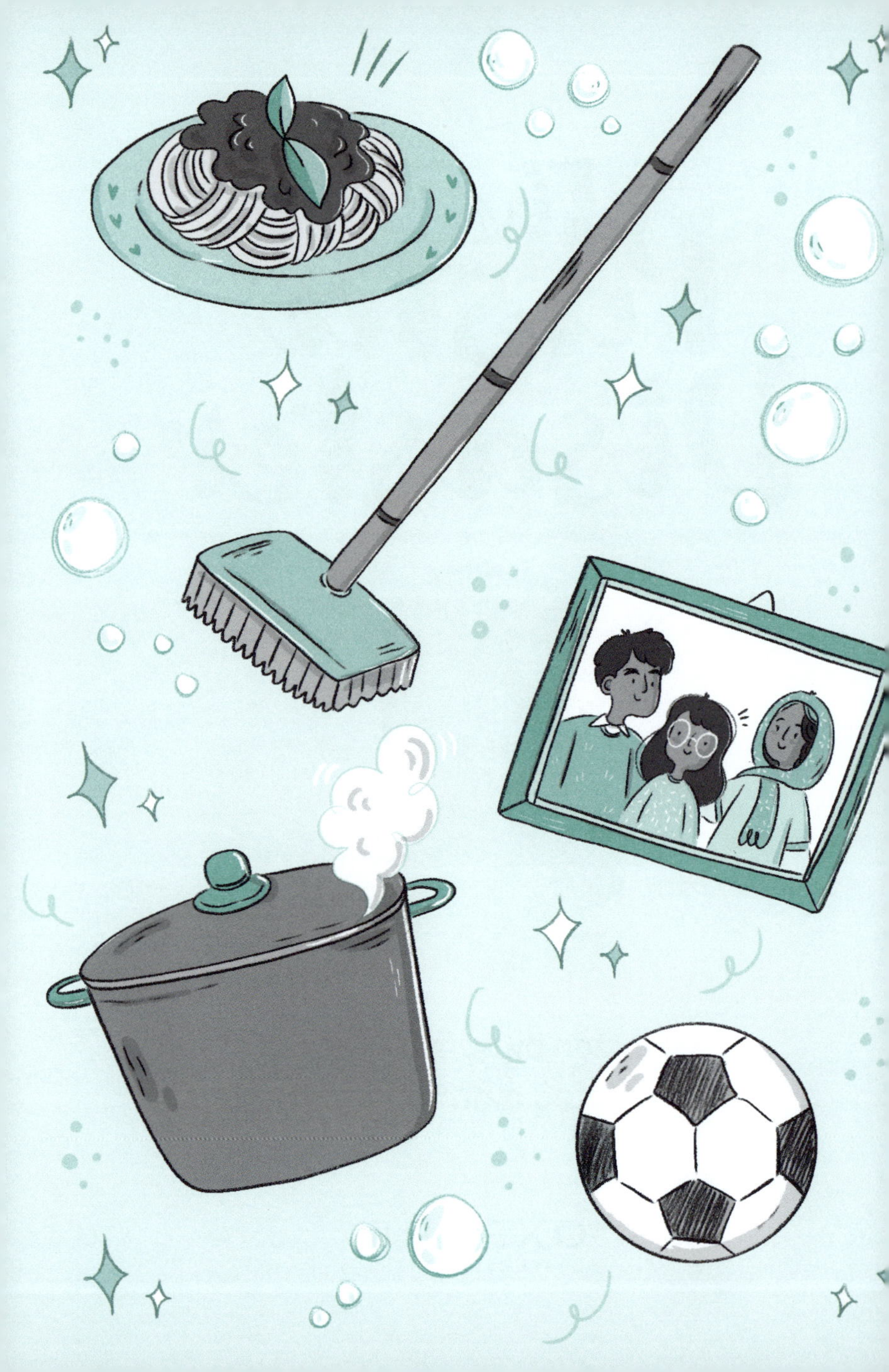

Read this book if ... you've ever been **ANNOYED by your FAMILY** and got into **TROUBLE.**

8

STOP AND THINK

In this book, Afsha is looking for a way to express her true feelings, but it doesn't go as planned.

What do you think might happen?

Meet the characters...

Mum

Afsha

Uncle Adam

In this book, Afsha calls her stepdad 'Uncle Adam'. Some children use 'Aunt' and 'Uncle' for adults they are not related to, as a sign of respect.

Chapter 1
The goal

'**GOAL!**' Uncle Adam was **YELLING** with joy. Afsha's book nearly fell out of her hands.

Afsha was sitting in her FAVOURITE SPOT, on the chair by the window. She was **trying** to read. However, she was **not** getting very far.

Uncle Adam was her new stepfather.

He had married Afsha's Mum recently and moved into their house.

Afsha thought Uncle Adam was very **messy**. His laptop and books were always **scattered** on the surfaces. He left his jumpers and socks **everywhere**, too.

Worst of all,

football was

always

on the TV.

'Did you see that goal, Afsha?' Uncle Adam asked. 'The striker has a unique ability.'

Afsha shook her head. She kept her eyes **glued** to her book. She didn't want to talk about football players kicking balls into nets.

Afsha wanted to read in peace. She wanted things to be like before. She **missed** the time when it was just her and Mum.

Afsha's father had died when she was four. She didn't really have many **memories** of him.

Afsha had always been the centre of Mum's world.

They did **everything** together.
Up until Uncle Adam had come along.

Then things had changed.

Last week, Mum asked Afsha if she wanted to call Uncle Adam 'Dad'! Afsha shook her head. She had a **real** dad. She didn't need another one.

Look back

1. What facts have you found out about Uncle Adam in this chapter?

2. How does Afsha feel about Uncle Adam?

3. What do you think Afsha could do about it?

Chapter 2
The dinner

The next day after school, Afsha ran home. She was **excited**. Her **best friend** Lily had invited her to dinner.

Mum was in her room, tidying up.

'Can I go to Lily's for dinner?' Afsha asked.

'Not today,' Mum said.

'But why not?' Afsha asked.

Mum smiled. 'Uncle Adam is making his **special pasta dish** today. We're going to eat as a **family**.'

'But I want to eat at Lily's house!' Afsha said.

'No buts, Afsha,' Mum said firmly.

Afsha **stomped**

back down to the living room.

Afsha rang Lily to say that she couldn't come to dinner. Then she switched on the TV. However, she couldn't concentrate. She was too **wound up**.

'What's so **special** about Uncle Adam's pasta dish anyway?'

Afsha muttered to herself.

*Why should I **miss out** on a fun time with Lily?* she thought. *Anyway, we're **not** a family! So how can it be a family meal?*

Uncle Adam was trying too hard to be her dad. Afsha wished he would **stop**.

Afsha did not need a new dad!

Uncle Adam's laptop beeped.
More noise!
Uncle Adam rushed into the room. He had to join a video call.
Afsha **scowled**.

'Hi Kevin!' said Uncle Adam. 'Is it crucial that we talk about the work now? I've just put the pasta on for the family meal.'

Afsha **rolled** her eyes.

Now Uncle Adam was telling people they were a **family**! If only she could think of a way to make him **stop**.

Just then, **she had an IDEA.**

She had to do it **before** Uncle Adam ended his call.

Look back

1. What do you think Afsha is going to do?

2. Do you think Afsha is right to be angry? What advice would you give her?

3. Why doesn't Afsha need a new dad?

Chapter 3
The pasta

Afsha tiptoed to the kitchen.

She **HURRIED** to the cooker where the pasta was cooking. She lifted the lid off the big pot. Her glasses got covered in steam. Afsha waved the steam away. She peered into the pot.

The water was almost boiling. Afsha paused. It seemed such a **good idea** a few minutes ago! However, now she **wasn't so sure**.

A **roar** of laughter came from the living room. Afsha jumped.

Uncle Adam was just so **loud**.
It was so **annoying!**

Afsha placed the lid on the counter. Her mind was made up. There was **no time** to waste.

She had to do it now.

Afsha opened the cupboard. Then she carefully **scooped** washing powder into a small plastic bowl. She held it over the pot. The water was near boiling point now.

Afsha closed her eyes and

poured it all in.

Afsha knew that the combination of **powder** and **boiling water** would bubble out of the pot. It would make the pasta unsafe to eat. Dinner would be **ruined**.

Afsha placed the lid back on the pot. Then she ran out of the kitchen.

Afsha's **heart** was **banging** in her chest. She closed her bedroom door. Mum was sure to be **furious**.

A few minutes later, Afsha heard Mum's angry voice.

'Afsha! Come down at once!' Mum shouted.

Afsha's heart was still **beating wildly**.

Afsha had ruined dinner for a reason. This was her chance to tell them **why**.

She had tried to hint before that she wasn't happy, but no one **ever** listened to her.

Look back

1. What do you think about what Afsha did?

2. Why does Afsha find Uncle Adam so annoying?

3. Find a word in Chapter 3 that means 'walked quietly'.

Chapter 4
'He's not my dad!'

There was **soapy water** all over the floor.

'Did you do this, Afsha?' Mum's voice was cold with anger.

Afsha took a deep breath.

She nodded. 'I did do it,' she said.

'**Why?**' Mum demanded.

'Because he's **not** my dad

and I wish he would **stop** acting like it!' Afsha shouted.

Mum's shoulders slumped.
Afsha had never seen Mum look
so sad.

'Mum ...' she hesitated.
Afsha hadn't expected Mum to look like she was going to **cry**.

'Please go to your room,' Mum said. She turned away.

Afsha trudged upstairs.

An awful feeling was **rising up** inside her. Afsha tried to ignore it. It felt like guilt, and she didn't understand why. She had only told the truth about her feelings.

Telling the truth was a **good** thing, wasn't it?

The next morning there was **no sign of Uncle Adam** anywhere in the house. He was **still missing** when Afsha came home from school.

After dinner, Afsha sat down to read in her favourite spot.

The silence felt good.

There was **still no sign** of Uncle Adam the next day, or the day after that.

In fact, **three whole days** passed without him. There were clear benefits – the house was tidy. Afsha wondered if Uncle Adam had left them **forever**.

All three days, Mum was quiet. Afsha thought she still looked a bit sad. Well, it was up to Afsha to **cheer** Mum up.

Look back

1. Do you think Afsha is glad she told the truth about how she felt? Why or why not?

2. Does Afsha regret Uncle Adam leaving?

3. Think of a few different words to describe how Afsha's mum might be feeling.

Chapter 5
A surprise

Afsha decided that Saturday would be a *mother-daughter day*.

'Mum, shall we go to the park today?' Afsha asked. 'Then we could get an ice cream.'

Mum shook her head. 'I'm **too busy** with work right now.'

'Oh ...' Afsha's face fell.

'Maybe next weekend,' Mum said.

Afsha couldn't help thinking about Uncle Adam. He would have **loved** to have gone to the park.

Uncle Adam would have even taken her to the cinema. They always munched on a **big box of sweet popcorn** together.

Afsha bit her lip, saying nothing. She would just wait for Mum to be **less busy**.

Afsha sat down to read her book, but she couldn't **concentrate**, even though there was silence in the living room.

Afsha frowned. She tried to work out why she was feeling like this.

'I thought I'd be **happy** if Uncle Adam left,' Afsha said to herself. **'But I'm not.'**

Afsha couldn't **believe** what she was feeling.

Afsha missed Uncle Adam!

The next morning, Afsha knew what she had to do.

'I have something to say,' she told Mum. 'I'm sorry that Uncle Adam has left us ... and ...

I wish he was back.'

Mum put her arm around Afsha.

'He left because I said

I didn't want him to be my dad,'

Afsha said.

'I feel very **ashamed** of how I behaved now. I wish I could apologize to him,' Afsha continued.

Mum hugged Afsha.

'I'm sorry too,' Mum said.

Afsha looked up at Mum. Did this mean Mum **understood** how Afsha had felt?

'I should have given you more time to get used to Uncle Adam. Instead, I forced us to act like a family **immediately**,' Mum said.

Just then, they heard a familiar voice.

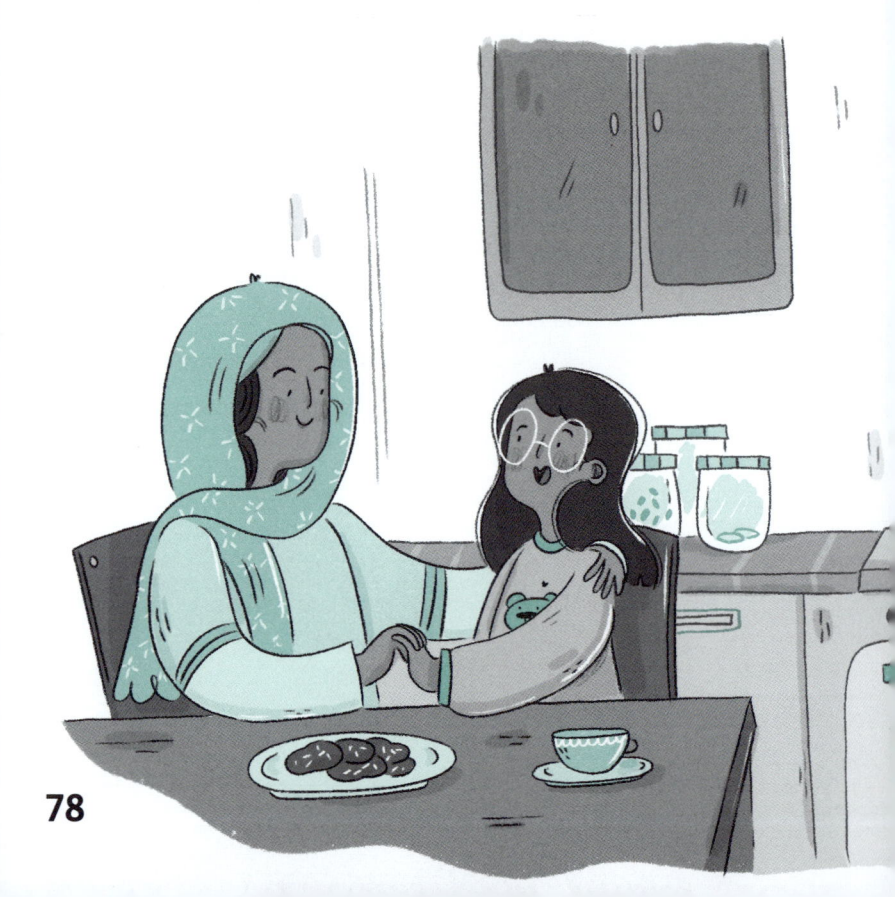

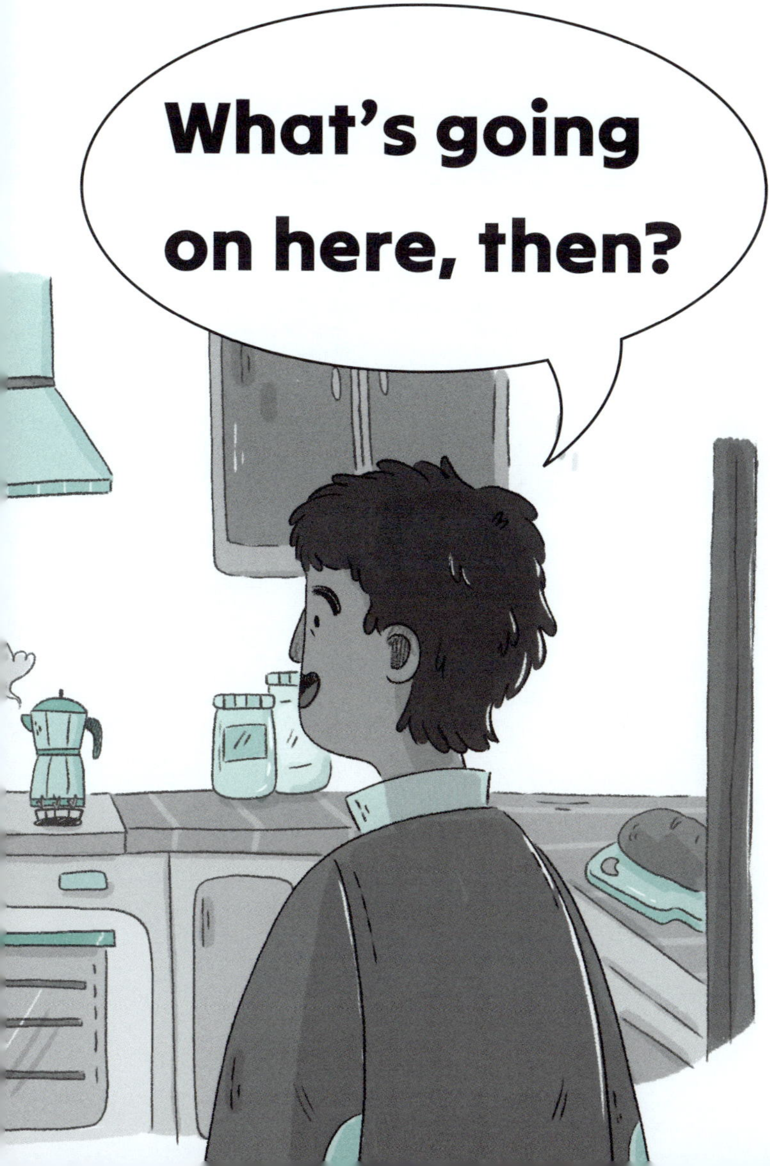
What's going on here, then?

Afsha's mouth fell open like a fish.

'I'm so glad you came back!' Afsha cried.

Uncle Adam looked confused. 'My work trip was only for a few days.'

'I thought you'd left us because of the **horrible** thing I said,' Afsha blurted. 'I'm sorry!'

'Today can be a **fresh start**,' Uncle Adam said.

Afsha took a deep breath.
'Can I call you Papa?'
Uncle Adam's eyes lit up.
'I'd like that.'

Uncle Adam wrapped his arms around Afsha and Mum.

'**Our family**,' Afsha said, *beaming*.

Look back

1. How have Afsha's feelings about Uncle Adam changed during the story?

2. How did Afsha feel when Uncle Adam came back?

3. Why do you think Afsha asks if she can call Uncle Adam 'Papa'?

Ha! Ha!

What did Mum Pasta say to Kid Pasta?

It's pasta your bedtime!

Read out loud

Here is a play called 'Talking to a Friend'. It is a conversation between Afsha and her friend Lily. Have you ever performed a play before?

Find a friend and decide which part you will play.

Read the whole play to yourself and think about how your character would speak. What tone will you use?

Practise the play together before you perform it.

Talking to a Friend

play

Lily: Why don't you like your Uncle Adam?

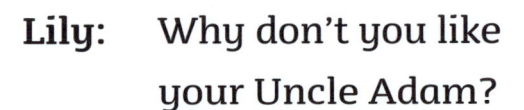

Afsha: I don't want him to be my dad.

Lily: He takes you to the park and the cinema every weekend.

Afsha: That's because he's trying to be my dad.

Lily: I don't think having a new dad means you replace the old one.

Afsha: I'm not sure I want him as my second dad.

Lily: It just means you're lucky to have another dad that loves you.

Afsha: I suppose so …

Read it again

1. After performing the play, discuss with your friend how you could both make it even better.

2. Try swapping roles and performing it again.

3. Then try memorizing your part so that you can say it without needing the book.

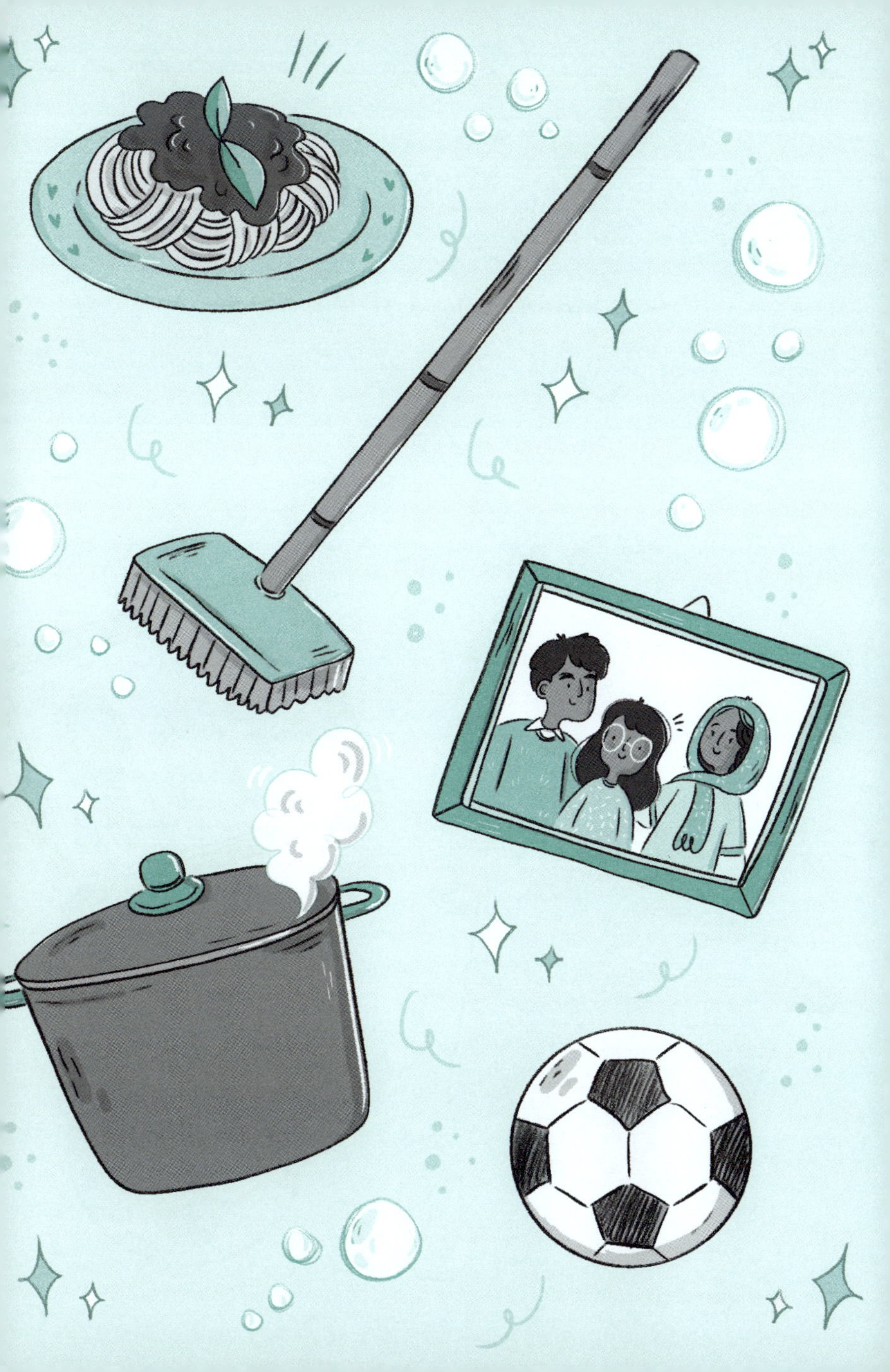

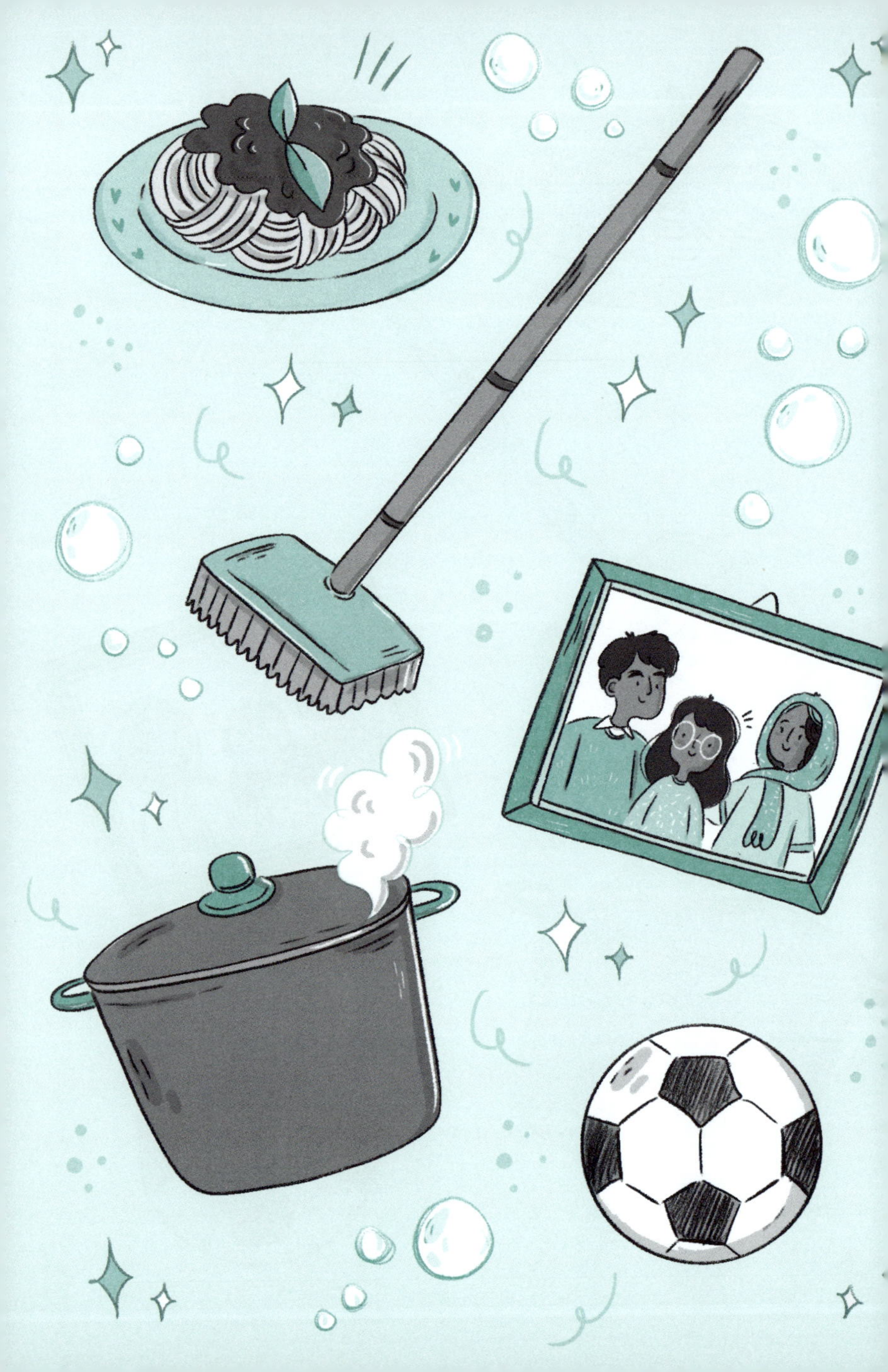

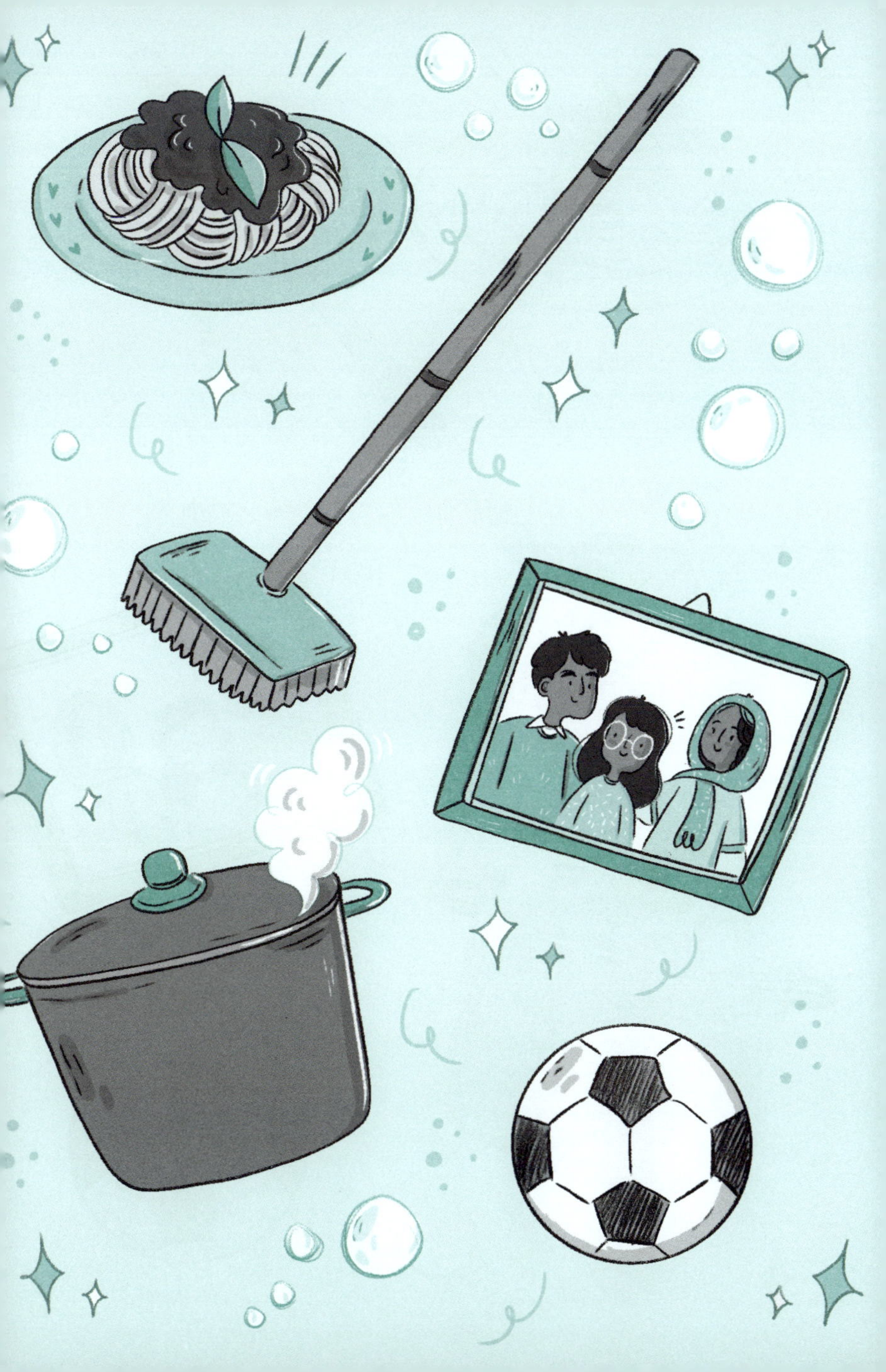

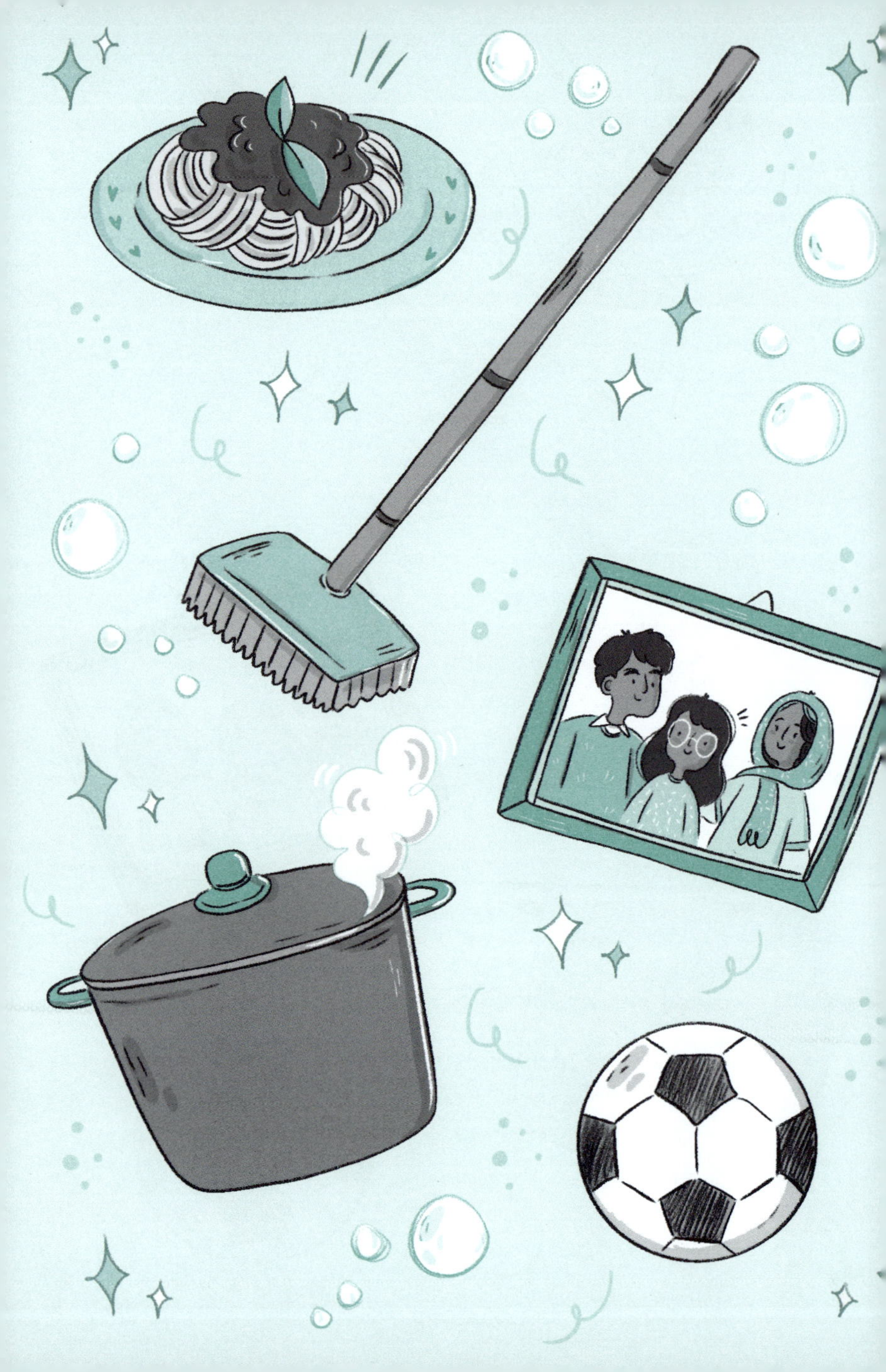